Extreme

FLY-
BOARDING

Virginia Loh-Hagan

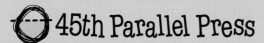
45th Parallel Press

Published in the United States of America by Cherry Lake Publishing
Ann Arbor, Michigan
www.cherrylakepublishing.com

Content Adviser: Liv Williams, Editor, www.iLivExtreme.com
Reading Adviser: Marla Conn, ReadAbility, Inc.
Photo Credits: ©Sebastian Marko/Red Bull Content Pool, 5; ©Robert Hoetink/Shutterstock.com, 6; ©Per Agge/Red Bull Content Pool, 8; ©Jörg Mitter/Red Bull Content Pool, 11; ©Enriquecalvoal/Dreamstime.com, 13; ©Enriquecalvoal/Dreamstime.com, 15; ©inffr-09/INFphoto.com/Corbis, 17; ©Clement Morin/Dreamstime.com, 19; ©serge mouraret/Demotix/Corbis, 21; ©muratart/Shutterstock.com, 23; ©FPW/Alamy Stock Photo, 24; ©Gabriel-m/istockphoto.com, 27; ©Svetlin Ivanov/Dreamstime.com, 29; ©Trusjom/Shutterstock.com, multiple interior pages; ©Kues/Shutterstock.com, multiple interior pages

45th Parallel Press is an imprint of Cherry Lake Publishing.

Library of Congress Cataloging-in-Publication Data

Names: Loh-Hagan, Virginia.
Title: Extreme flyboarding / by Virginia Loh-Hagan.
Description: Ann Arbor : Cherry Lake Publishing, [2016] | Series: Nailed it! | Includes bibliographical references and index.
Identifiers: LCCN 2015049730| ISBN 9781634710909 (hardcover) | ISBN 9781634711890 (pdf) | ISBN 9781634712880 (paperback) | ISBN 9781634713870 (ebook)
Subjects: LCSH: Flyboarding--Juvenile literature.
Classification: LCC GV840.F59 L65 2016 | DDC 797.5--dc23
LC record available at https://lccn.loc.gov/2015049730

Printed in the United States of America
Corporate Graphics Inc.

ABOUT THE AUTHOR

Dr. Virginia Loh-Hagan is an author, university professor, former classroom teacher, and curriculum designer. She loves to ride Jet Skis; she's not sure about flyboarding. She lives in San Diego with her very tall husband and very naughty dogs. To learn more about her, visit www.virginialoh.com.

Table of Contents

About the Author 2

CHAPTER 1:
Super Flyboarders 4
CHAPTER 2:
Flying High 10
CHAPTER 3:
Newest Sport on the Block 16
CHAPTER 4:
Figuring Out Flyboarding 22
CHAPTER 5:
Thrills and Spills 26

Did You Know? 30

Consider This! 31

Learn More 31

Glossary 32

Index 32

Super Flyboarders

Who are some famous flyboarders? What makes them special to the sport?

Nellie Kubalek is 40 feet (12 meters) in the air. She lands a backflip. It took three days of training to learn. She's the top U.S. female flyboarder. Not many females **flyboard**. She teaches girls to flyboard. She created a special group. It's called FlyGirlz of Florida.

She can do double backflips. She's training to do triple backflips. Only a few people can do it. She said, "I want to be one of the first ladies to accomplish it."

She loves flyboarding. It came easily to her. She was a gymnast for 16 years. She said, "I just took to it and kept on going."

Damone Rippy is a flyboarding champion. He started at age 14. He's the youngest professional flyboarder.

He watched online videos. He tried flyboarding at a friend's birthday party. He got hooked. He trains several times a

Flyboarders perform in many shows around the world.

Flyboarders are sometimes called riders.

week. He performs amazing stunts. He flies over 40 feet (12 m) above water.

Rippy said, "The higher I go, the higher the risk. You fall harder and are more uncontrolled." He hasn't had any major injuries. But he has hurt his ribs. He's hurt his back. He has cuts. He has bruises.

He said, "I want to push the limits and continue to do my very best. I love this sport."

Jordan Wayment started as a professional wakeboarder. He competed at age 14. Then, he started flyboarding. He could go higher. He could do more tricks.

Spotlight Biography: Suksan "Liw" Tongthai

Suksan "Liw" Tongthai is from Bangkok, Thailand. He's the 2014 X Dubai Flyboard World Cup Champion. He's also the 2013 Flyboard World Cup Champion. He invents new tricks. He's the first flyboarder to land a triple backflip. He flyboards higher than others. He flyboards faster than others. Before flyboarding, he played soccer and takraw. Takraw is a Thai sport. It combines Hacky Sack and volleyball. He wanted a change. He tried flyboarding. He pushed himself as a beginner. He had an accident. He said, "I hit my leg really hard on the hose because I didn't understand everything yet. I hurt my leg so bad and had to go to the hospital for a small surgery. I was forced to stop training for 2 months to recover. But was thinking about it every day. As soon as I healed up, I was back out there."

Flyboarders are passionate about their sport.

He was the first to do flyboarding tricks. He said, "Once I finally landed the first backflip, then everyone else started landing backflips. Then, we started spinning and doing double frontflips." He crashed and learned. He flyboards every day.

He said, "You have no barriers. You have the whole sky. So there are no limits." He's a world champion. He's competed in several contests. He's taught over 200 people to flyboard.

"You have no barriers. You have the whole sky. So there are no limits."

Flying High

How does flyboarding work? What do flyboarders need? How do flyboarders learn to flyboard?

A flyboard is like a water jet pack. It looks like a small snowboard. It's hooked to a hose. The hose is hooked to a Jet Ski. The Jet Ski powers the flyboard. It pumps water into the flyboard. Water goes straight to flyboarders' feet. The hose **propels** flyboarders into the air. Propels means pushes up. This allows flyboarders to fly. They **hover**. Hovering means floating.

Flyboarders work with Jet Ski **pilots**. Pilots are drivers. Flyboarders use hand motions. They tell pilots which tricks they want to do. They are careful about landing. They land safely away from the Jet Ski.

Advanced flyboarders can control their own Jet Skis. They use a remote control.

The Jet Ski pilot controls the water pressure. Flyboarders control height levels. They do this by balancing on the board.

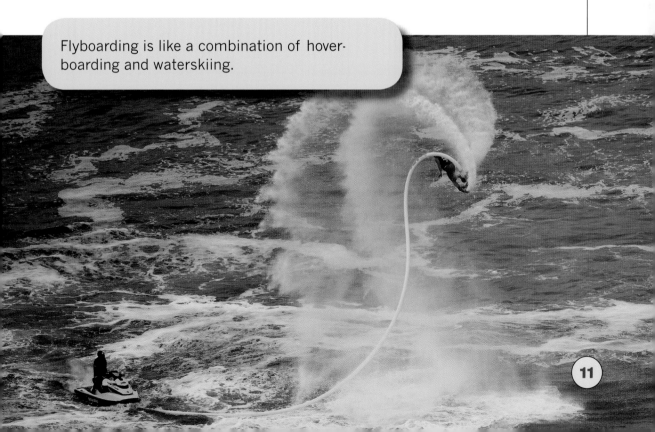

Flyboarding is like a combination of hover-boarding and waterskiing.

Extreme Flyboarding: Know the Lingo

720: two consecutive spins while increasing in height

Backflip: single backflip without the board touching the water

Barrel roll: adding a twist in the air while diving forward

Dead man drop: cutting off power while the flyboarder is flying

Dog chain: diving so high and aggressively that the hose snaps the flyboarder back, causing a belly flop

Dolphin dive: diving forward into the water

Huge dolphin: dolphin dive done from heights of 20 feet (6 m) or more

Layout backflip: backflipping where the flyboarder opens up and holds the position until landing

Missile: a half rotation on a backflip leading to a vertical dive with headfirst entry

Reverse dolphin: diving backward into the water

Slalom: moving the flyboard side to side

Superman: flying forward

Thread the needle: backflipping and then diving through the loop of the hose

Flyboarders need to be in water at least 13 feet (4 m) deep.

Flyboarders can go 45 feet (13.7 m) high. They shoot out of the ocean. They fly into the sky. They spin. They flip. They twist. Then, they dive back into the water. They're flung headfirst through the waves. They look like dolphins. Many flyboarding moves are named after dolphins.

Flyboarders stand on flyboards. Their feet are in boots and bindings. Bindings are like straps. Their hands control **stabilizers**. Stabilizers control their flights. Flyboarders wear helmets. They wear life jackets.

Flyboarding is easy to learn. It takes 2 to 5 minutes to learn to stand and fly. But it's hard on the body. Flyboarding is a **vertical** water sport. This means flyboarders go straight up. Human bodies aren't meant to do that. They're not meant to fly. This puts stress on their bodies.

Callon Burns is a flyboarding champion. He believes in having confidence. He believes in building body strength. He does short, intense workouts. He trains his body to recover from **fatigue**. Fatigue means getting tired. He said, "Like athletes across all sports, you must stay consistent and dedicated to taking care of your body."

"Flyboarding is a vertical water sport."

There is a difference between recreational and competitive flyboarding.

Newest Sport on the Block

Who invented flyboarding? How did it develop into a competitive sport?

Flyboarding was invented by Frank Zapata. It was invented in 2012. It's a new action water sport.

Zapata is French. He's a Jet Ski racing champion. He invented the flyboard. He was on a family vacation. He imagined a flying wakeboard. He realized his Jet Ski was powerful. It produces enough power to lift a person.

He needed a special **device**. The device had to climb out of water. It had to be stable in the air. A device is a machine or tool. He came up with the flyboard. He presented it at a Jet Ski world championship. It was a success.

Francois Rigaud likes extreme sports. He discovered flyboarding online. He said, "When I saw a clip, I knew I had to try it. It is the jet pack of today. It's new. And it's a real rush."

He runs a flyboarding shop. He said, "Having been

Zapata posted his invention online. The response was instant and global.

snowboarding and surfing, it's a totally different feeling because you're actually flying."

He helped bring flyboarding to the United States. He rented

Advice from the Field: James Bissett

James Bissett owns a flyboarding company in Long Island, New York. He's a professional flyboarder. He's had over 25 hours of training. He learned about safety, gear, skills, and instruction. He started as a wakeboarder and kite surfer. Now, he skydives. Skydiving gives him the balance to fly. It also helps him understand how the flyboard works. He said, "It's like any other sport. You need to practice. And the more time you do, the better you get." He had to get used to the speed. Then, he could do tricks. He enjoys pioneering the sport. He likes connecting with other flyboarders. He said, "I am looking to make great friendships ... we can all work together and make this sport something great!"

Because flyboarding is a new sport, social media has helped to develop it.

out flyboarding gear. He made flyboarding videos. He took flyboarding photographs. He **mentored** flyboarders. He coached young people in the sport.

Flyboarding became more than a hobby. In 2012, it became a sport. The first flyboarding World Cup was held in the Middle East. Zapata showed off his flyboarding skills. He put on a water light show.

The flyboarding World Cup is held each year. The world's top flyboarders compete against each other. It has become a grand event.

More competitions popped up. There's the North American Flyboard Championship. There are competitions in Japan, Thailand, and other countries.

Flyboarding has become a **spectator** sport. Spectators are audience members. People come to see flyboarders. They cheer. They clap.

The World Cup draws competitors from more than 20 countries.

Figuring Out Flyboarding

What are some concerns about flyboarding? What are some ways cities have tried to regulate flyboarding?

Flyboarding has become popular. Many people are excited about it. But some aren't.

Fishermen and scientists wonder about the effects. They worry about fish and coral. Bob Richmond is a scientist. He's from the University of Hawaii. He's worried about the noise. Fish avoid noisy areas. Flyboards are noisy.

Dr. Richmond has another worry. Fish eggs get pumped through the hose. This kills them.

William Aila is a state official in Hawaii. He knows flyboarding is exciting. He said, "But you got to look beyond the excitement."

Some worry about the safety of the sport. They worry about people getting hurt. Flyboarders practice unsafe moves. They dive-bomb into the water. They could hit moving boats. They could hit swimmers. They could hit piers.

Flyboarding as a recreational sport is popular in Hawaii, California, Florida, and Mexico.

There needs to be more research on the effects of flyboarding.

Cities are coming up with new rules. They want to prevent accidents. They don't allow flyboarding within 100 feet (30.5 m) of objects. They require flyboarders to be in at least 6 feet (1.8 m) of water. They require flyboarders to wave orange flags. This is to warn others.

Justin Wood owns a flyboarding company. He said, "This is a brand new sport. There's nothing wrong with **regulation**." Regulation means having rules.

That Happened?!?

Students played Frisbee while flyboarding! They're from Montgomery Bell Academy in Nashville, Tennessee. They played Frisbee with professional flyboarders. The students tossed the Frisbee from a bridge. Flyboarders were in the river. They caught the Frisbee. They made a video of it. The video became very popular. Watson Dill was one of the students. He said, "It was on *SportsCenter* and that was crazy. And my whole family was watching it. So to see that video and be a part of it was just incredible." The stunt was McClain Portis's idea. He was sitting on the couch. He was looking through social media. He e-mailed the flyboarding company. He wanted to do something nobody else had done. Portis said, "It's kind of something we can do for fun to just get out there and stay off the video games."

Thrills and Spills

How is flyboarding safe? What are examples of flyboarding accidents?

Since flyboarding began, there haven't been major injuries. Flyboarders wear safety gear. They travel with a Jet Ski pilot. So, someone is always there to help. Sometimes flyboarders lose control. Flyboards **absorb** impact. They take a lot of the fall.

But accidents do happen. A 15-year-old girl was flyboarding. She was in a river in Wales. The tides changed. She got trapped. She was between a Jet Ski and the flyboard. She was underwater. She was under for more than 5 minutes.

A lifeboat rescued her. She was given first aid. A helicopter came. It took her to the hospital.

Two men were flyboarding. They were in Utah. They got in an accident. They both got hurt. One was the flyboarder. He dived into the water. He tried to avoid the Jet Ski. He hit

Even nonswimmers can flyboard. They have to wear life jackets.

the water. He flipped over the Jet Ski. He broke his leg. The other man was the Jet Ski pilot. The Jet Ski landed on him.

When Extreme Is Too Extreme!

Flyboarders move like dolphins. Seabreachers are more extreme. They move like sharks! The Seabreacher X is a special watercraft. It's like a shark with rockets strapped to its fins. It has a supercharged 300 horsepower engine. It has half the power of a Lamborghini. It can travel 50 miles (80.5 kilometers) per hour. It can dive 16 feet (5 m). It can skid above or dive below the water. It uses its fins to turn quickly. It can do special moves. It can breach. It can do barrel rolls. It can jump straight out of the water. Other models are designed to act like dolphins or orcas. But the shark version is the best. It has the best balance. It handles the best. It can do more extreme stunts. Seabreachers are more expensive than flyboards. They can cost over $80,000.

Because flyboarding is new, most tricks have not been named yet.

His brain was injured. Rescue workers found them. They took them to the hospital.

Flyboarding is an extreme sport. It requires speed and height. It can be dangerous. Flyboarders live on the edge. But they need to be smart!

Did You Know?

- Most flyboards have a weight limit. The minimum weight is 100 pounds (45.4 kilograms). The maximum weight is 300 pounds (136 kg).

- Leonardo DiCaprio was seen flyboarding. He was in Ibiza, Spain. Justin Bieber also flyboarded in Ibiza.

- Flyboarders shouldn't go deeper than 8 feet (2.4 m). Doing so can cause ear pain.

- Flyboarders can't drop too quickly. This can burst their eardrums.

- Frank Zapata said, "Being on a flyboard is the closest I'll ever get to being Iron Man." Iron Man is a fictional superhero.

- A flyboard costs over $7,000. (Jet Skis are also expensive.) Since 2012, fewer than 3,000 flyboards have been sold. Hotels and instructors are the biggest flyboard buyers.

- People with serious back or knee injuries should be careful. They should reduce the power on the flyboard.

- Most companies require flyboarders to be at least 16 years old. Parents must give permission.

- Motoaki Suzuki won the first ever Japan Flyboard Cup. Suzuki came in first place. He's part of the Crazy Ninjas. It's Japan's flyboarding team.

Consider This!

TAKE A POSITION! Do you think flyboarding is safe or dangerous? Argue your point with reasons and evidence.

SAY WHAT? Explain how flyboarding combines elements of other extreme sports.

THINK ABOUT IT! Flyboarding is an expensive sport. This means not many people can do it. Some would say it's an elitist sport. What do you think about this?

SEE A DIFFERENT SIDE! Reread Chapter 4. How do scientists feel about flyboarding? Do you see their point? Do you think the negative effects of flyboarding are worth it?

Learn More: Resources

PRIMARY SOURCES

Up in the Air, a short flyboarding documentary film (2014), https://www.youtube.com/watch?v=fAEH7e4ZNNo.

SECONDARY SOURCES

Ditton, Lia. *50 Water Adventures to Do Before You Die: The World's Ultimate Experiences In, On, and Under Water*. London: Adlard Coles, 2015.

Gigliotti, Jim. *Water Sports*. Chicago: Heinemann-Raintree, 2012.

WEB SITES

Atlantic Flyboard: http://www.atlanticflyboard.com

H2RO Magazine—Flyboarding: http://www.h2romagazine.com/flyboard-magazine-official

Glossary

absorb (ab-ZORB) to take in

device (di-VISE) a machine or tool

fatigue (fuh-TEEG) getting tired

flyboard (FLYE-bord) to practice a water sport that uses a jet-powered board

hover (HUHV-ur) to float

mentored (MEHN-tord) to have coached young people

pilots (PYE-luhts) drivers

propels (pruh-PELZ) pushes up

regulation (reg-yuh-LAY-shuhn) having rules

spectator (SPEK-tay-tur) an audience member

stabilizers (STAY-buhl-eye-zurz) a tool that controls the flight of a flyboard

vertical (VUR-ti-kuhl) going straight up

Index

accidents, 26–29

competitions, 9, 19, 20, 21

equipment, 13

flyboarding
  concerns about, 22–25
  famous flyboarders, 4–9
  history of, 16–21
  how it works, 10–15
  rules, 24–25

injuries, 6, 7, 23, 26–29, 30

Jet Skis, 10–11, 16, 26, 28

lingo, 12

rules, 24–25

safety, 23, 26–29

Seabreachers, 28

training, 4, 14

tricks, 4, 6, 7, 9